Just ADD *Color*

DAZZLING PATTERNS

BARRON'S

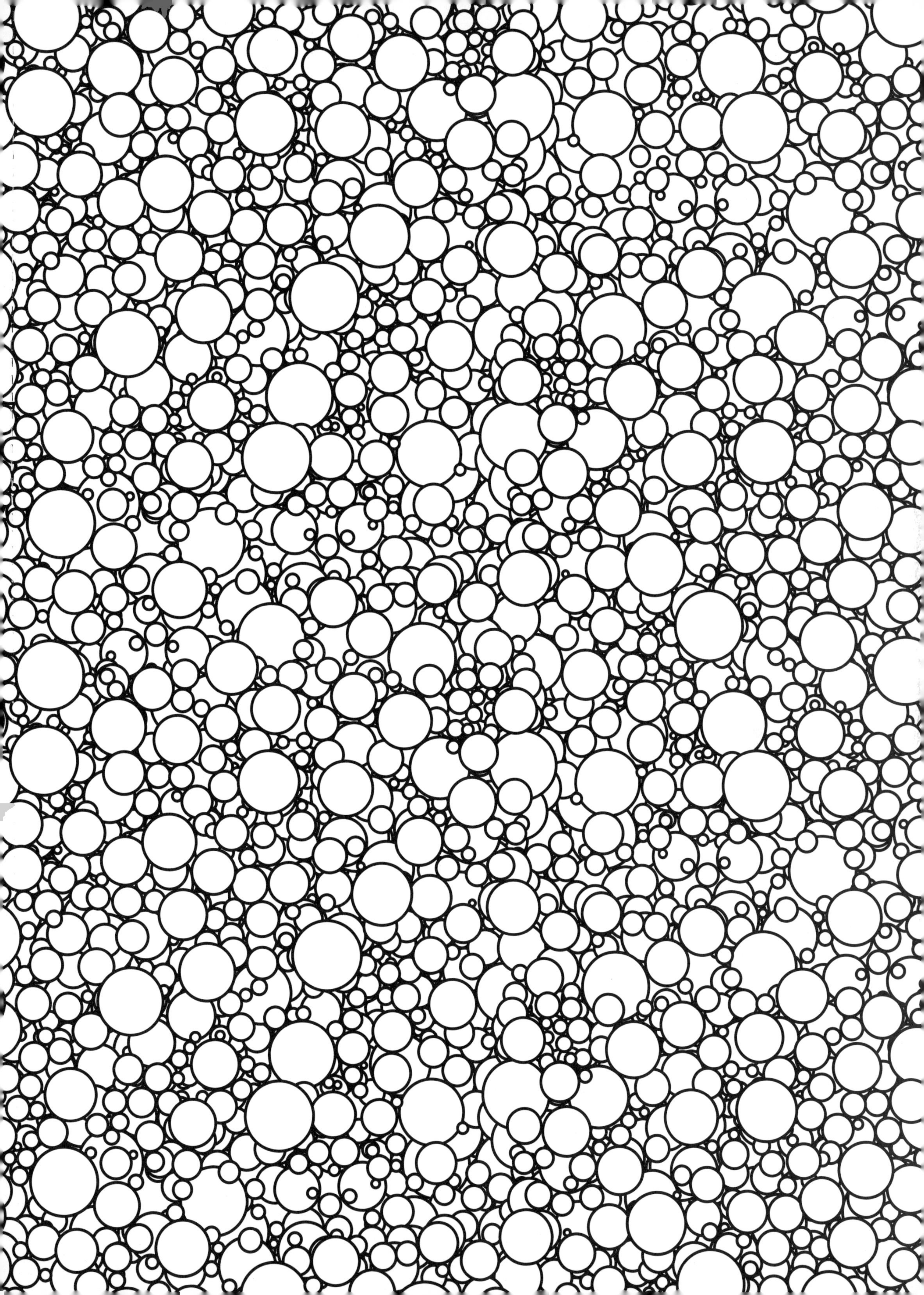

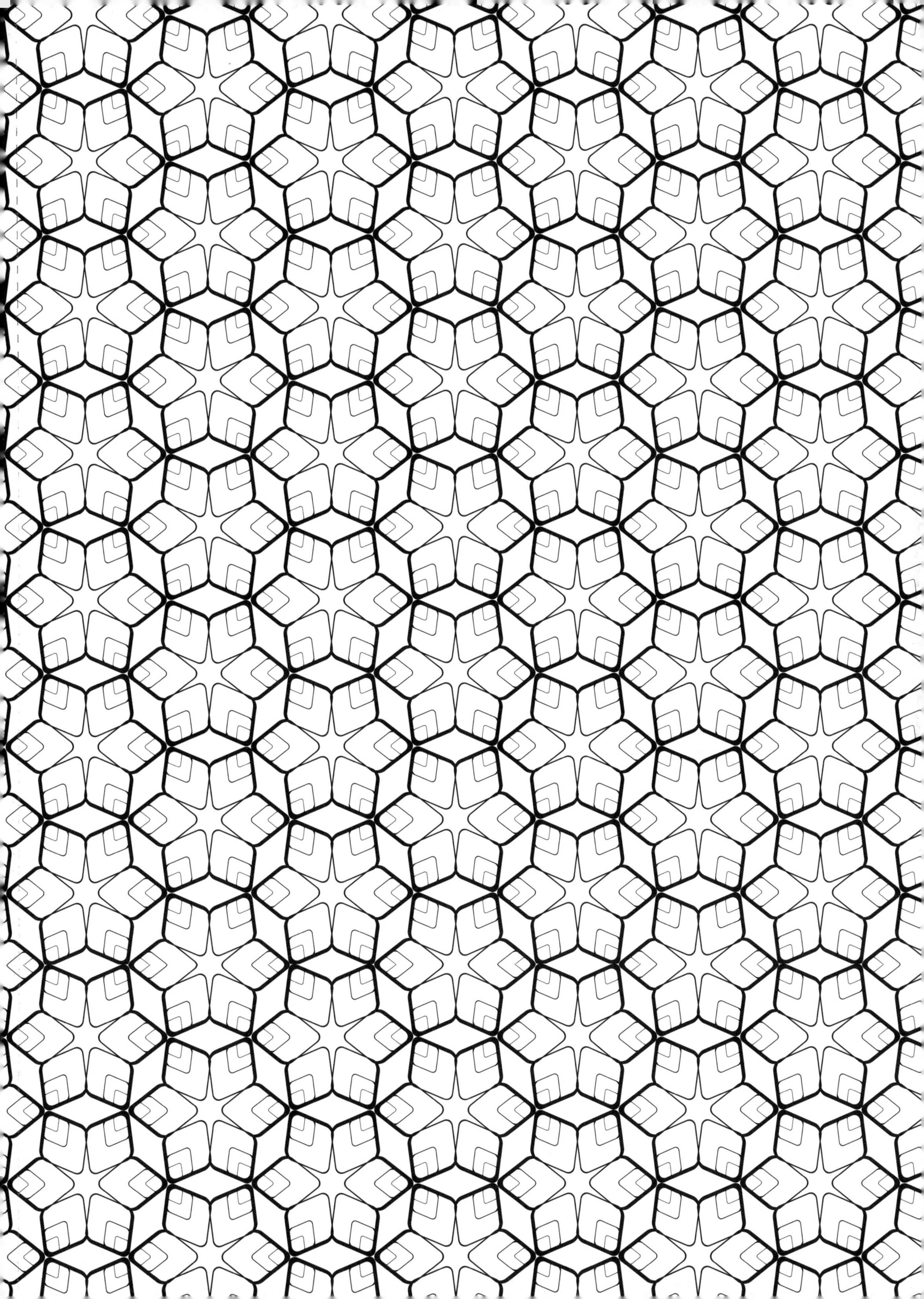

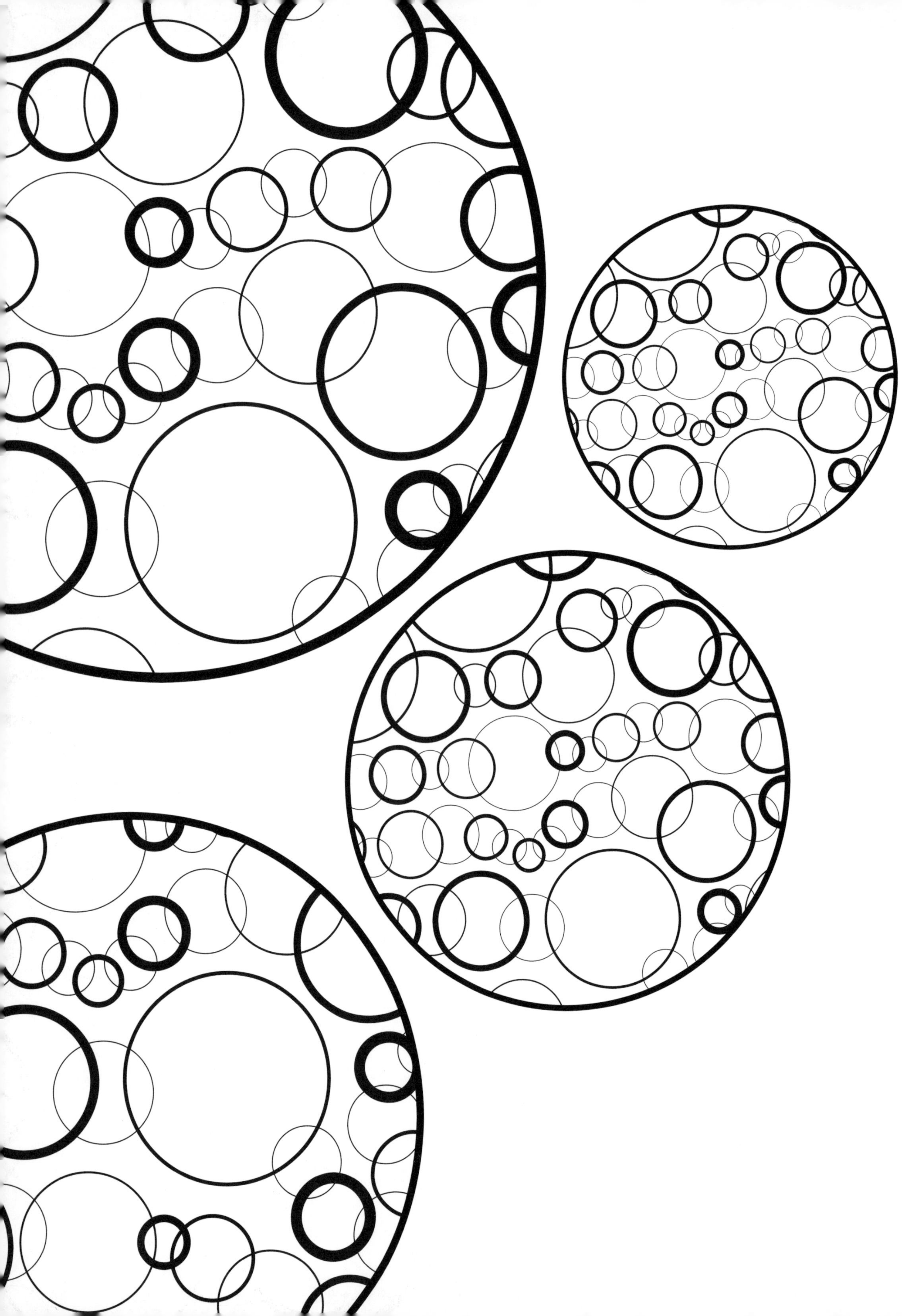

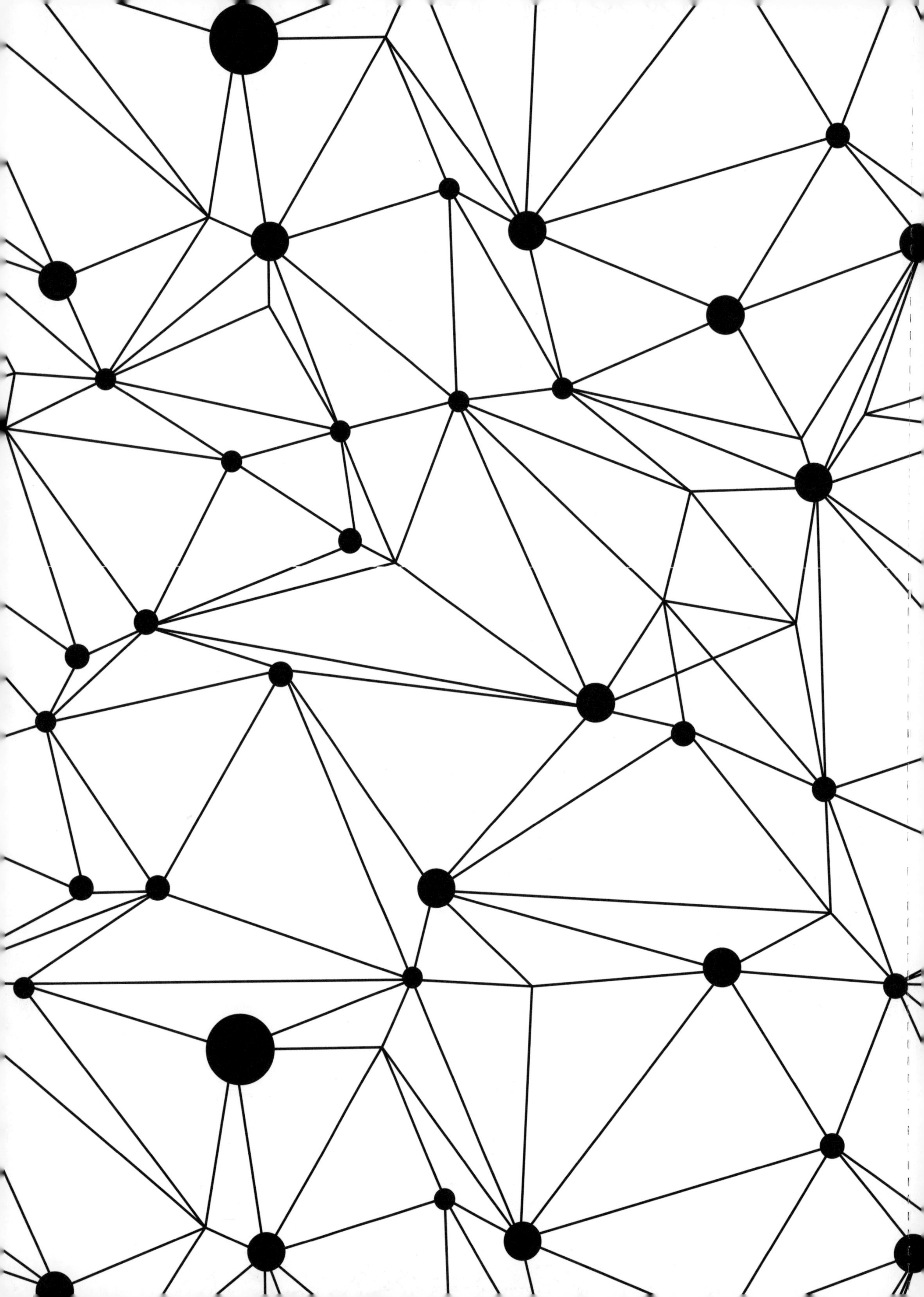

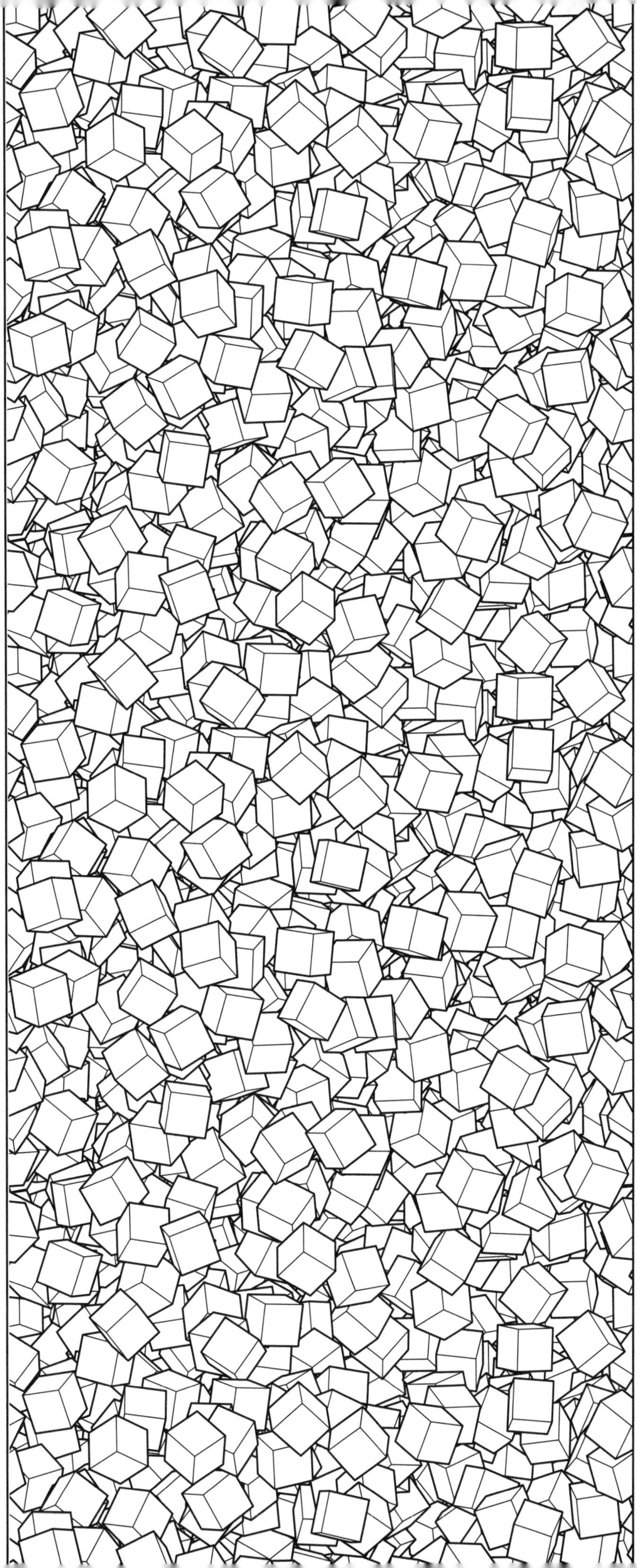

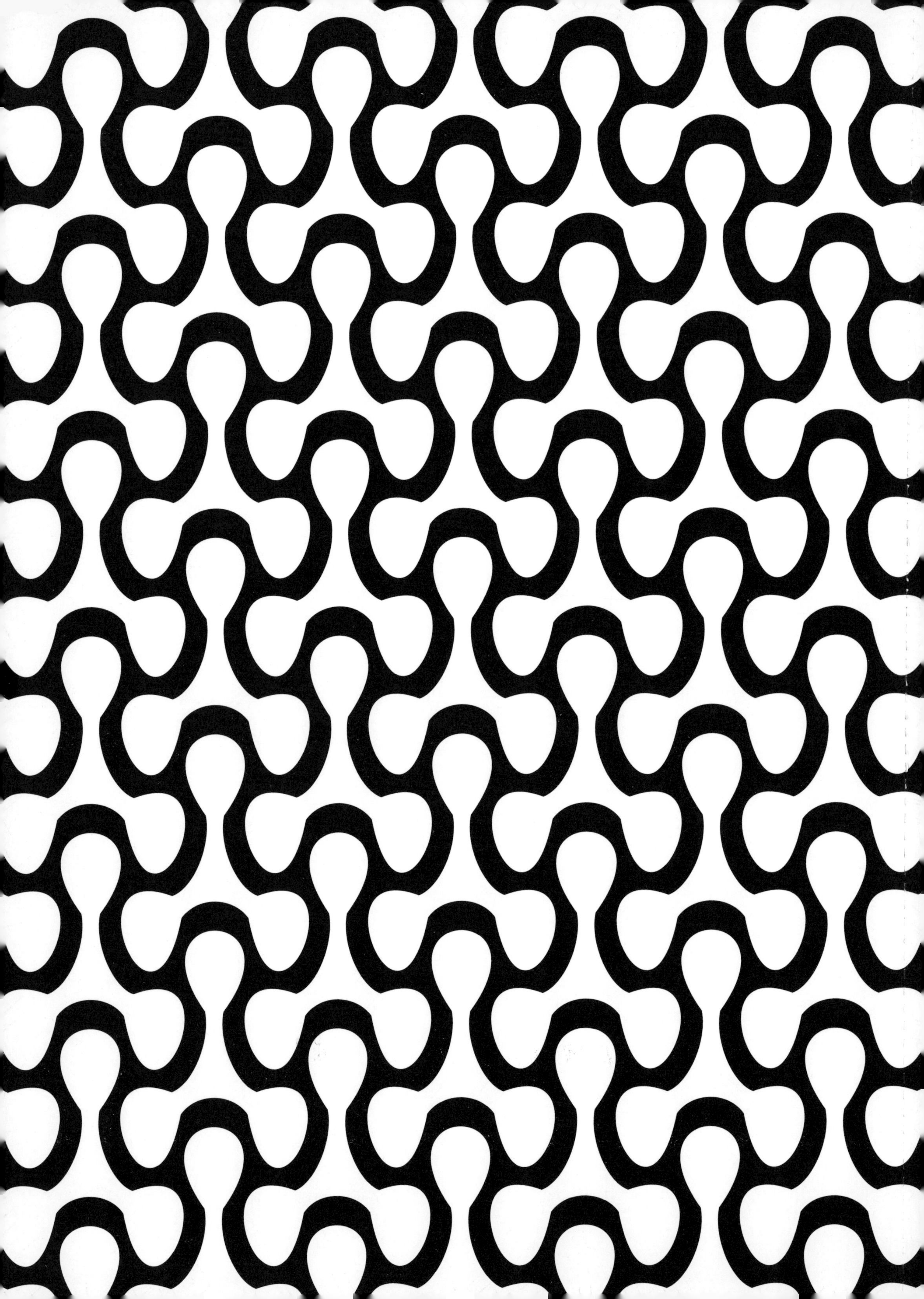

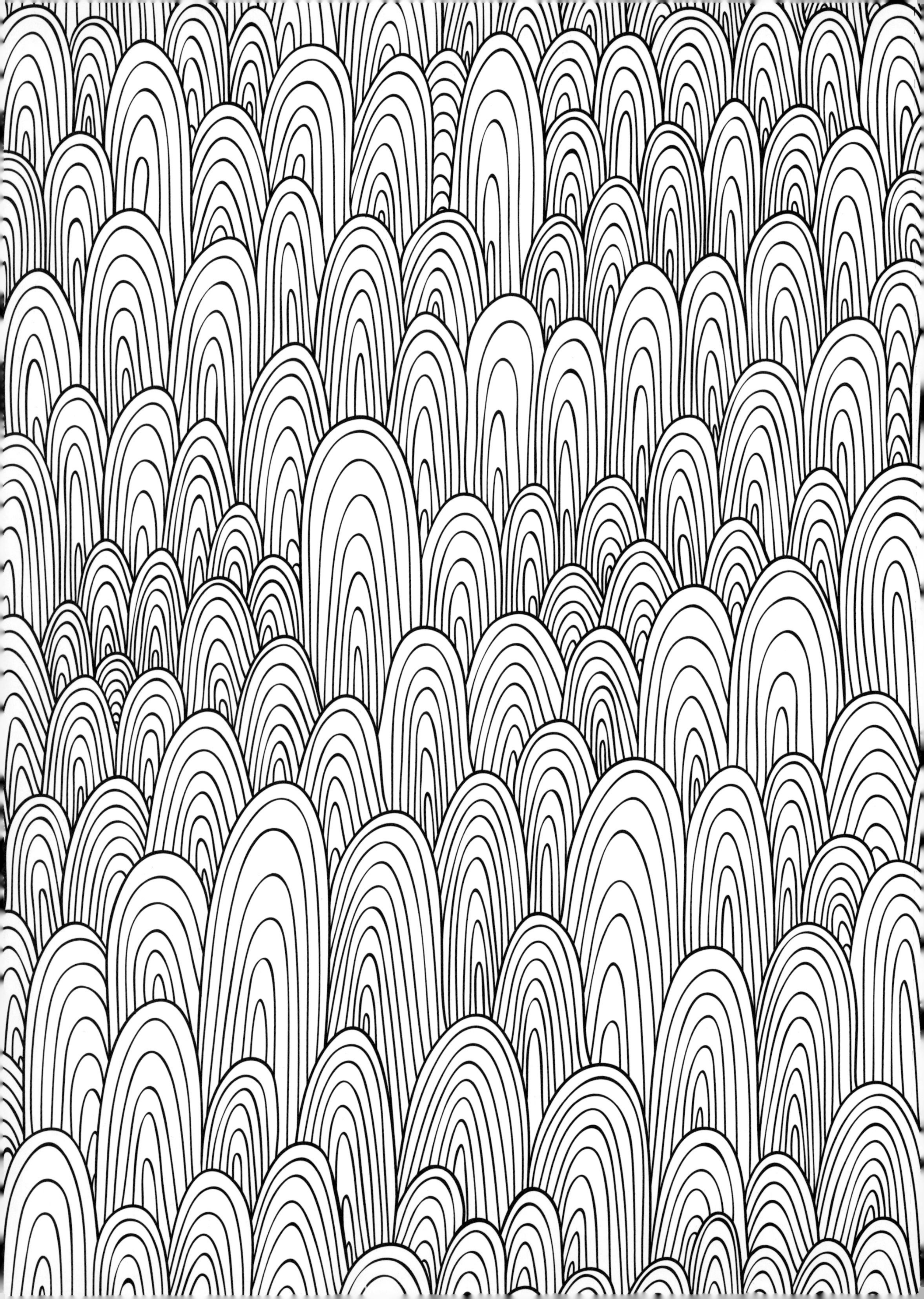

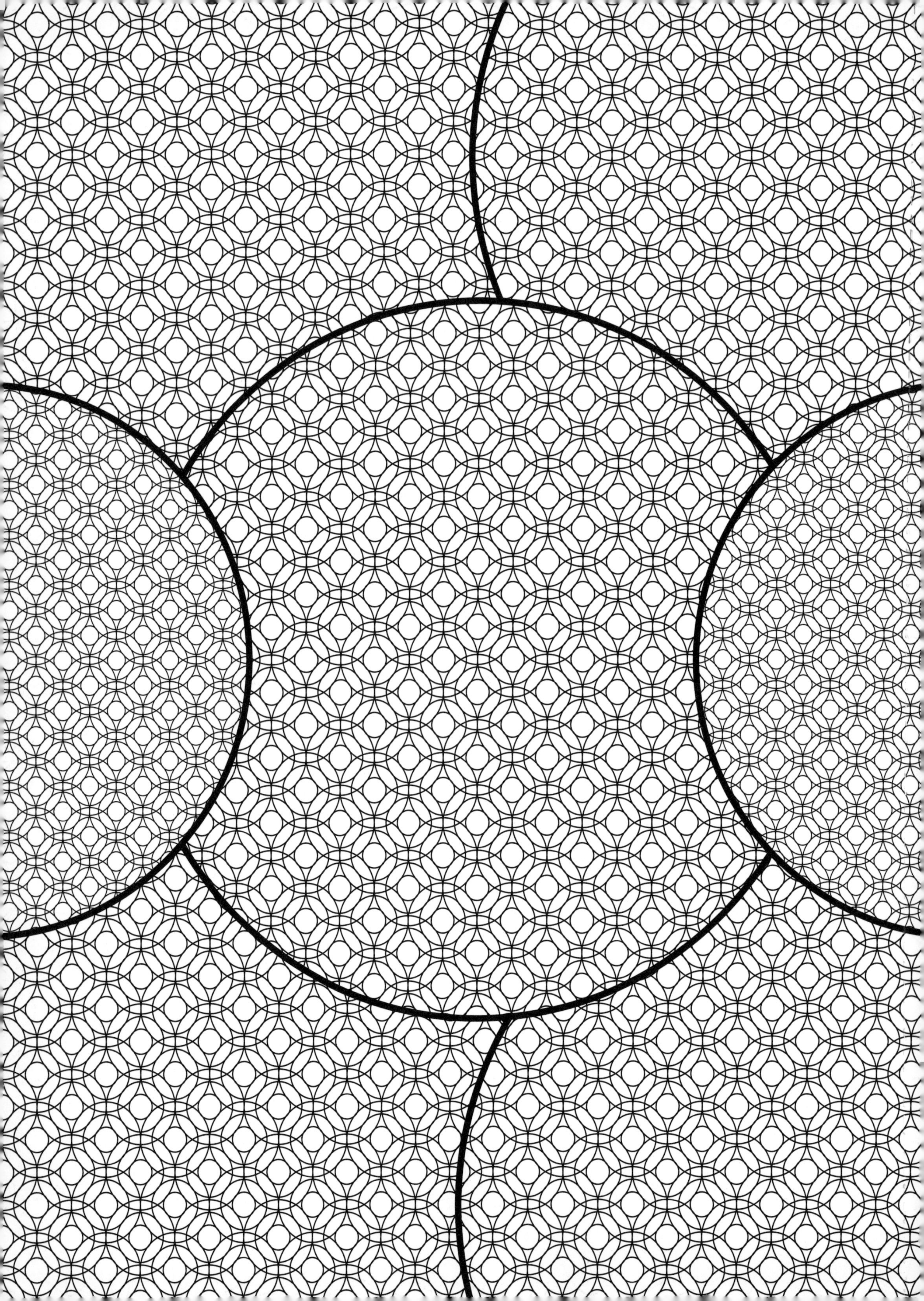

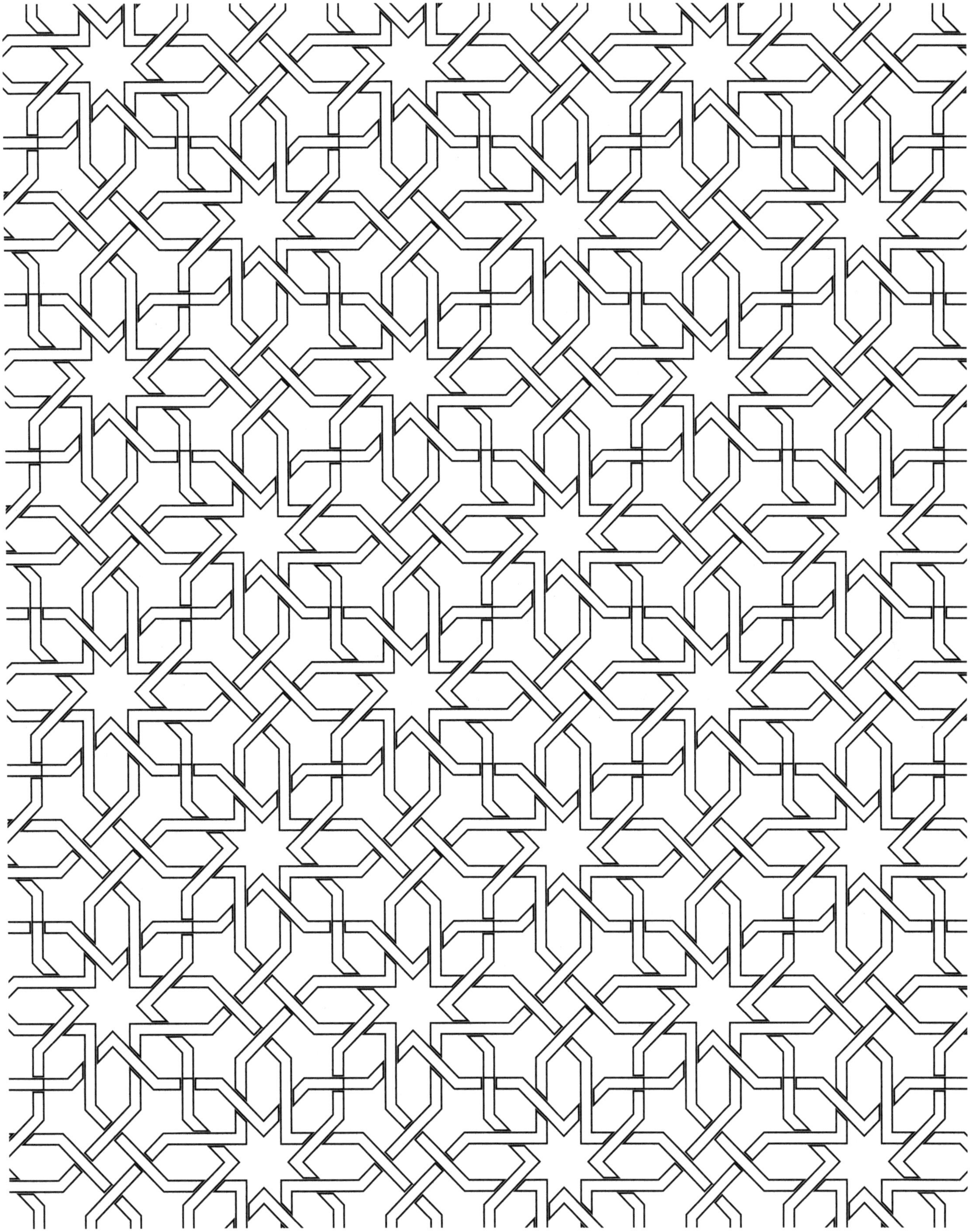

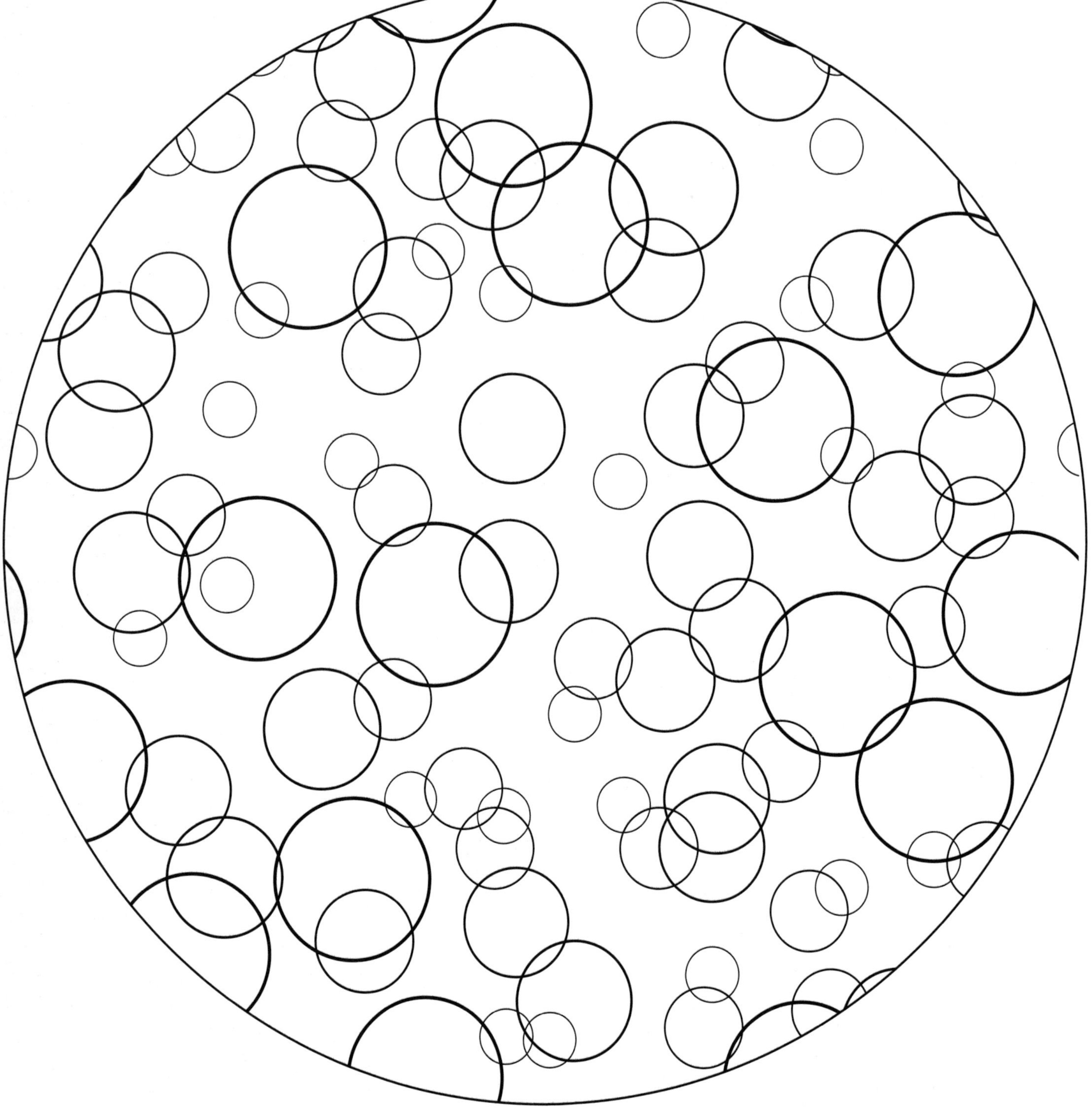

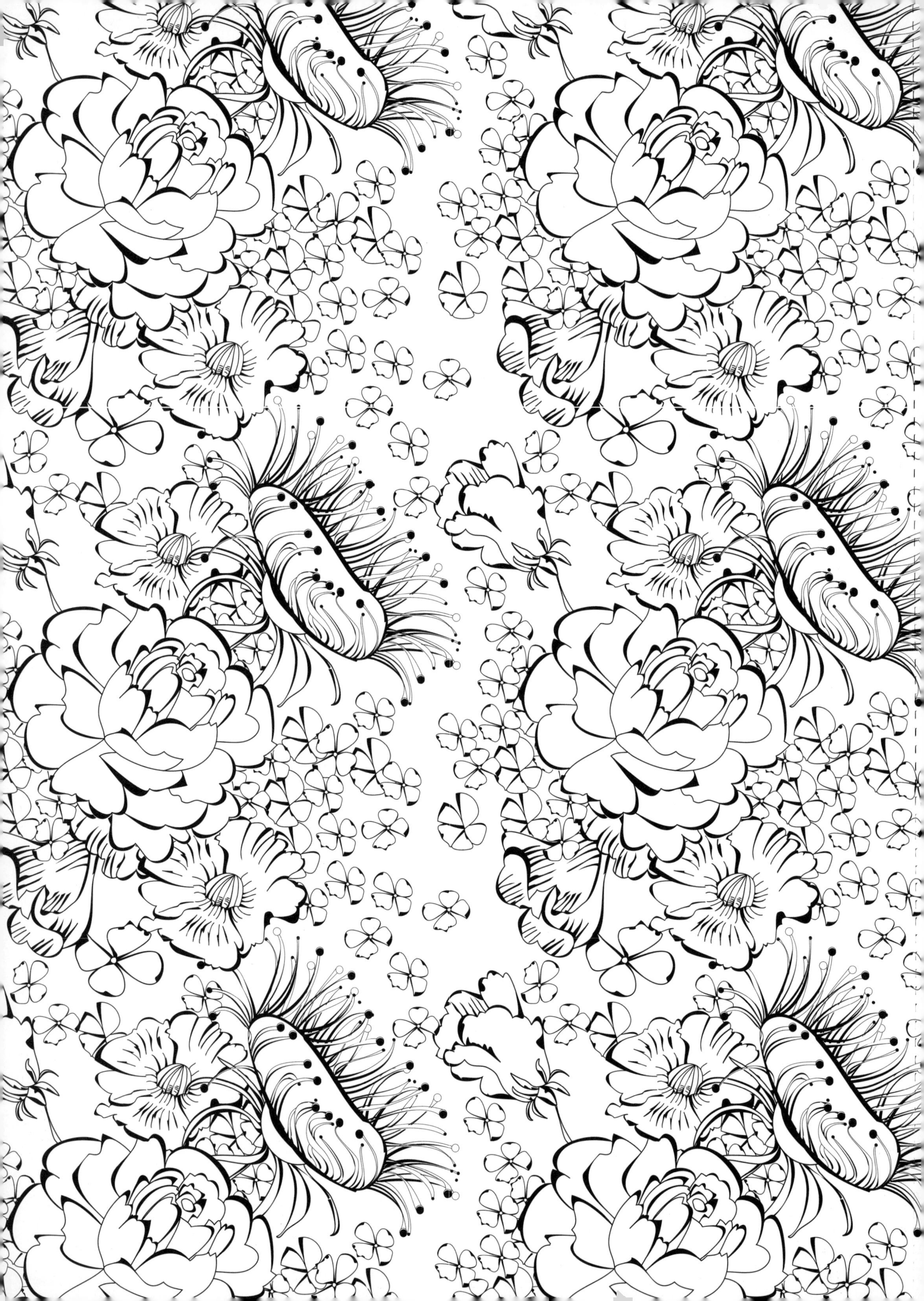

First edition for North America published in 2015 by Barron's Educational Series, Inc.

All inquiries should be addressed to:

Barron's Educational Series, Inc.
250 Wireless Boulevard,
Hauppauge, New York 11788

www.barronseduc.com

ISBN: 978-1-4380-0611-6

Library of Congress Control Number: 2014939397

Manufactured by: RRD Asia, Dongguan, China

Printed in China

9 8 7 6